Income Inequality
and IQ

T0266231

Income Inequality and IQ

Charles Murray

THE AEI PRESS

Publisher for the American Enterprise Institute

WASHINGTON, D.C.

1998

Distributed to the Trade by National Book Network, 15200 NBN Way, Blue Ridge Summit, PA 17214. To order call toll free 1-800-462-6420 or 1-717-794-3800. For all other inquiries please contact the AEI Press, 1150 Seventeenth Street, N.W., Washington, D.C. 20036 or call 1-800-862-5801.

ISBN 0-8447-7094-9

1   3   5   7   9   10   8   6   4   2

THE AEI PRESS
Publisher for the American Enterprise Institute
1150 17th Street, N.W., Washington, D.C. 20036

ISBN 978-0-8447-7094-9

Contents

FOREWORD, *Christopher DeMuth*   vii

1 INTRODUCTION   1

2 INCOME INEQUALITY AND IQ FOR ADULTS IN THEIR LATE TWENTIES AND EARLY THIRTIES   5

3 PARENTAL SOCIOECONOMIC STATUS AND IQ AS COMPETING EXPLANATIONS FOR ECONOMIC SUCCESS   9

4 ANALYSIS OF SIBLINGS IN THE NATIONAL LONGITUDINAL SURVEY OF YOUTH   12

5 HOW MUCH DIFFERENCE DOES IT MAKE WHETHER THE ANALYSIS CONTROLS FOR PARENTAL SES OR COMPARES SIBLINGS?   24

6 THE UTOPIAN SAMPLE   29

NOTES   45

ABOUT THE AUTHOR   49

Foreword

This study is one of a series commissioned by the American Enterprise Institute on trends in the level and distribution of U.S. wages, income, wealth, consumption, and other measures of material welfare. The issues addressed in the series involve much more than dry statistics: they touch on fundamental aspirations of the American people—material progress, widely shared prosperity, and just reward for individual effort—and affect popular understanding of the successes and shortcomings of the private market economy and of particular government policies. For these reasons, discussions of "economic inequality" in the media and political debate are often partial and partisan as well as superficial. The AEI series is intended to improve the public discussion by bringing new data to light, exploring the strengths and weaknesses of various measures of economic welfare, and highlighting important questions of interpretation, causation, and consequence.

Each study in the series is presented and discussed in draft form at an AEI seminar prior to publication by the AEI Press. Marvin Kosters, director of economic policy studies at AEI, organized the series and moderated the seminars. A current list of published studies appears on the last page.

CHRISTOPHER DEMUTH
President, American Enterprise Institute

1

Introduction

What causes income inequality? The usual answers are economic and sociological. Capitalism systematically generates unequal economic rewards. Social class distinctions create different opportunities in life, leading to unequal economic rewards.

These sources of inequality are undoubtedly important, but economists and sociologists have tended to discuss them in a vacuum, ignoring the personal characteristics that individuals bring to the economic marketplace.

Psychologists group such characteristics under the heading of *individual differences,* embracing all aspects of social and cognitive functioning in which the unit of measurement is the individual rather than any group identity such as gender, occupation, ethnicity, or social status. Industriousness is an individual difference. So are other hard-to-measure characteristics such as charm, honesty, creativity, and courage.

In this monograph I discuss one of the most important of the individual differences, intelligence. Specifically, I will be discussing the kind of intelligence measured by IQ tests: mental quickness, the ability to process complex information accurately, to draw inferences, extrapolate, and interpolate. This capacity is not to be confused with common sense or wisdom. What an IQ score distills into a number, with impressive statistical reliability and validity, is the constellation of qualities that people generally have in mind when they use the word "smart" to describe someone.

Intelligence and Income

In thinking about the relationship of intelligence to a person's income, a few things are apparent from everyday life. The first is that IQ has a highly irregular relationship to income. A few of the occupations that require a high IQ, notably medicine and law, are also known for their high incomes, but many of the others provide good incomes that top out well below wealth. The professoriate, for example, more than half a million strong, is drawn almost exclusively from the top 10 percent of the IQ distribution, but its members get professors' salaries. Meanwhile, an entrepreneur with an average IQ but a hot idea can make millions.

We also observe from everyday life that, beyond a certain level, the relationship of IQ to professional success is inconsistent. The most successful partner in the law firm is not necessarily the smartest; the finest surgeon draws upon many skills other than raw mental processing ability. The most successful in these occupations would also rank high on an IQ test, but seldom at the farthest reaches of the right-hand tail of the bell curve.

Within the world of business, the relationship of IQ to income becomes still more uncertain. Some corporate jobs have become cognitively more demanding—the R&D and financial sides of business are examples. But as often—sales is a good example—qualities other than IQ still dominate in determining who makes a fortune.

So if you are looking for a simple explanation of income inequality, IQ is not it. But important statistical relationships do not require simplicity. Modest correlations can have large social consequences, and so it is with IQ and income. If you are trying to understand how the dynamics of income inequality have played out in the past few decades, and will continue to play out in the decades to come, IQ is an indispensable piece of the puzzle.

In *The Bell Curve,* the late Richard J. Herrnstein and I discussed these issues in part one, "The Emergence of a Cognitive Elite."[1] We made these large points, accompanied by extensive documentation:

• Over the course of the century, concentrated in the past fifty years, education has become cognitively partitioned, with the most prestigious echelon of schools shifting from places for the socioeconomic elite to places for the cognitive elite.

• Over the course of the century, concentrated in the past fifty years, the proportion of people in the top IQ decile gaining entry into high-IQ occupations has increased dramatically.

• IQ is one of the best single predictors of job productivity.

• During the last half of the century, the economic value of IQ in the marketplace has increased.

• All the technological and economic forces that led to these developments may be expected to continue into the next century.

In part two, "Cognitive Classes and Social Behavior," we examined the relationship of IQ to a variety of social and economic outcomes such as poverty, unemployment, and family structure. Many of these outcomes bear on income inequality, but income inequality was no longer our topic. At no point in *The Bell Curve* did we try to use the National Longitudinal Survey of Youth (NLSY) to draw any direct conclusions about the magnitude of income inequality already apparent in the NLSY sample and the role that IQ might have played in producing it.

One purpose of this monograph is to fill in that gap. I then turn to a powerful method, not employed in *The Bell Curve,* of assessing the importance of IQ independent of all other family background factors. The monograph concludes with an exploratory analysis of the outer limits of reducing income inequality through success in social policy.

The Data and the Measures

The data are taken from the NLSY, one of the largest and best of the American longitudinal data bases. It began in 1979 with 12,686 subjects. The data presented here go through the 1994 interview wave, which means that the most recent calendar year with income data is 1993. All dollar figures are stated in 1993 dollars. The measure of IQ is the Armed Forces Qualification Test, 1989 scoring version, normalized for each year's birth cohort to an IQ metric with a mean of 100 and a standard deviation of 15 (NLSY subjects were born from 1957 through 1964). Details on both the NLSY and the AFQT may be found in *The Bell Curve,* appendixes 2 and 3.

2

Income Inequality and IQ for Adults in Their Late Twenties and Early Thirties

L et us begin with the first-order relationship between IQ and income. I employ a modified version of the cognitive classes we defined in *The Bell Curve,* cutting off the five classes at the 10th, 25th, 75th, and 90th percentiles of the normal distribution.[2] In the IQ metric, this means break points at scores of approximately 80, 90, 110, and 120. Descriptively, these classes are characterized in the following paragraphs.

Our point of departure is the group in the middle of the bell curve, those with a measured IQ somewhere from 90 through 109, whom we labeled *Normal.* Fifty percent of the American population falls in this category. Their intelligence easily permits them to be competent in all the core roles of family and community life and to pursue any occupation not requiring a college education. Most of them have difficulty in completing a college education (historically, the mean IQ of college graduates has been about 115), but some do so.

To their immediate right on the bell curve come the *Bright,* with IQs from 110 through 119, representing the 75th through 89th percentiles of the IQ distribution. Anyone with an IQ this high has the intellectual ability to get through college, though not necessarily in every major. This IQ range includes many of the most successful Americans.

The *Very Bright* have IQs of 120 and above. They represent the top 10 percent of the IQ distribution. Having an IQ this high is not necessary to become a physician, attorney, or business executive, but extra cognitive horsepower gives an edge in any occupation that draws heavily on the verbal and visuospatial skills measured by IQ tests.

Turning to the left-hand side of the bell curve: those adjoining the Normals are persons with IQs from 80 through 89, whom we labeled *Dull*. If the IQ score is accurate, someone in this range is unlikely to get through four years of college without special dispensations. Ordinarily, Dulls work at anything from low-skill jobs through lower-level white collar or technical jobs.

At the far left-hand side of the distribution are the bottom 10 percent of the IQ distribution, the *Very Dull*, with IQs under 80. These include the retarded, but many people with IQs in this range are neither retarded nor incapacitated. They find it difficult to cope with school, but can be productive employees at menial and semi-skilled jobs, and sometimes at skilled jobs as well if their shortfall in intellectual capacity is counterbalanced by other abilities.

Figure 2–1 shows an overview of the income of these five groups from 1978, when the subjects were aged between thirteen and twenty-one and mostly too young even to have an income, through 1993. The measure of income is median earned income (including salary, wages, and net income from a business or farm).[3]

At the beginning of the period shown in the graph, the medians for all the cognitive classes are extremely low, reflecting the many subjects who have reached legal working age but are still in school full time. Then fortunes begin to diverge. The median for the Very Bright, represented by the thick black line, begins to rise rapidly as the college years end and continues to rise thereafter, with a

FIGURE 2–1
MEDIAN EARNED INCOME BY COGNITIVE CLASS, 1978–1993
(thousands of $ 1993)

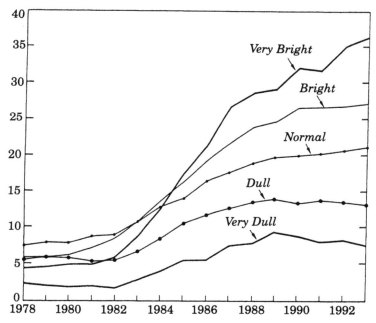

SOURCE: NLSY.

brief pause in 1991. At the other extreme, represented by
the thick grey line, is the median for the Very Dulls. It
peaks in 1989 and falls gently thereafter. By the end of
the period shown in the graph, when this group of young
adults has reached ages twenty-eight through thirty-six,
those in the top cognitive class have a median earned income 4.8 times the median of those in the bottom class.
The other cognitive classes are also clearly separated. By
1993, the Very Brights are earning 33 percent more than
the Brights, who in turn make 29 percent more than the
Normals, who in turn make 62 percent more than the
Dulls, who make 73 percent more than the Very Dulls.

A similar story emerges when total family income is
used as the measure. Table 2–1 summarizes the results for

TABLE 2–1
EARNINGS BY COGNITIVE CLASS, 1993
(1993 dollars)

Cognitive Class	Median Earned Income	Median Family Income
Very Bright (90+ centile)	36,000	55,700
Bright (75th–89th)	27,000	48,470
Normal (25th–74th)	21,000	40,200
Dull (10th–24th)	13,000	29,830
Very Dull (less than 10th)	7,500	19,100

SOURCE: NLSY.

the full NLSY sample. Cells have observations ranging from a minimum of 474 to a maximum of 3,059 observations.

The effect of including welfare payments and spouse's income (the two most common types of income added when total family income is the measure) is to narrow the proportional gaps among cognitive classes while tending to widen the raw dollar gaps. The regularity of the statistical relationship is similar for both measures. The bivariate correlation of IQ to income in this population of adults in their late twenties to mid-thirties was .37 for earned income and .38 for total family income.

The diverging lines in figure 2–1 vividly portray what Herrnstein and I meant by cognitive stratification. But is IQ really the explanation for these results? Many other possibilities come to mind. Perhaps education, not IQ, is the key: people with better educations are simultaneously enabled to get high incomes and high scores on IQ tests. Perhaps money and influence are the key: rich parents can procure both good educations and lucrative jobs for their lucky children, while poor parents can provide neither. Perhaps more subtle dynamics are at work—whether the child grew up with both parents, whether the child grew up in neighborhoods that encouraged achievement, and so on.

3

Parental Socioeconomic Status and IQ as Competing Explanations for Economic Success

The most straightforward competing explanation is that IQ and income are both products of parental socioeconomic status (SES). The general test of such hypotheses in the social sciences is a regression equation, in this case entering a measure of parental SES and the NLSY offspring's IQ as independent variables and the offspring's income as the dependent variable. In the analyses that follow, I use earned income as the dependent variable rather than family income, because earnings more directly reflect the subject's own abilities and effort. I have conducted parallel analyses for family income, which yield similar results.

In *The Bell Curve,* Herrnstein and I used an index to express parental SES, based on parental income, education, and occupation.[4] For parental education, we used the years of education of the more educated parent. Occupational prestige was measured with a widely used scale created in the 1960s by sociologist Otis Dudley Duncan.[5] Income was expressed as total family income from all sources. The index itself is expressed as a standardized variable with a mean of zero and a standard deviation of one. Table 3–1 shows the results when earned income in 1993 is regressed on IQ and the parental SES index for the full NLSY sample.

An extra IQ point is associated with an extra $462 in wages independently of parental SES. To compare the relative importance of the two variables, one may convert the coefficients into a common metric based on standard scores, shown under the heading "Standard Beta." The standardized regression coefficients round off to .10 for parental income and .31 for offspring's IQ. Whereas each variable has a statistically significant independent effect on the offspring's income, the magnitude of IQ's independent effect is about three times as large.

When dealing with IQ and parental socioeconomic status, how trustworthy are the results from regression analyses? Two contrasting objections may be raised. The first is that the variables used to represent parental SES are inadequate; the second is that the variables used to represent parental SES are confounded. In other words, regression analyses with independent variables representing "other explanations" may either underestimate or overestimate the independent role of IQ. They will overestimate the role of IQ insofar as important aspects of the child's background are omitted from the list of variables. They will underestimate the role of IQ insofar as the variables for the competing explanations (such as parental income) are themselves indirect expressions of the parents' IQ, which is in turn transmitted to the child through both genes and the environments that parents of varying IQs provide for their children.[6]

TABLE 3–1
REGRESSION ANALYSIS OF THE COMPARATIVE ROLES OF PARENTAL SES AND IQ ON OFFSPRING'S INCOME

Term	Estimate	Standard Beta	Standard Error	t-ratio	Significance level (Prob. > [t])
Intercept	− 22,333.89	—	1,836.0	− 12.16	<.0001
Parental SES	2,057.46	0.0982	263.26	7.82	<.0001
IQ	462.36	0.3136	18.52	24.97	<.0001

Summary statistics
Number of observations: 8,098
Dependent variable: earned income, 1993
R^2: 0.1433
R^2 adjusted: 0.1431

SOURCE: NLSY.

4

Analysis of Siblings in the National Longitudinal Survey of Youth

There is a way to cut this methodological knot. It controls not just for socioeconomic background but for the entire complex of variables that go into defining the environment in which a child grows up. It lends itself to complex analytic techniques, but at bottom it is both simple and intuitively persuasive: compare siblings who have grown up in the same home, with the same parents, but who have different IQs. I am indebted to Sanders Korenman of the City University of New York and Christopher Winship of Harvard University, who brought the possibilities of the NLSY in implementing this approach to my attention (the NLSY included in its sample 5,863 subjects who shared the same household with at least one other NLSY subject as brother or sister) and who conducted their own reanalysis of *The Bell Curve* using siblings, to which I will return.

To qualify for the sibling sample I use here, both siblings had to have a valid score on the Armed Forces Qualification Test (AFQT) administered in 1980. To make matching for background as unambiguous as possible, I further limited the sample to pairs of subjects who were full biological siblings and who lived in the same home

TABLE 4–1
IQ CHARACTERISTICS OF THE PAIRED SIBLING SAMPLE BY COGNITIVE CLASS

Cognitive Class	n	Mean IQ	Std. Dev.	Mean IQ Difference $(IQ_C - IQ_R)$
Very Bright siblings (90th + centile)	128	125.1	5.6	+ 21.8
Bright siblings (75th–89th)	326	114.0	2.7	+ 11.8
Normal reference group (25th–74th)	1,074	99.1	5.9	—
Dull siblings (10th–24th)	421	85.9	2.5	− 11.2
Very Dull siblings (less than 10th)	199	74.5	5.4	− 21.1

SOURCE: NLSY.

TABLE 4–2
SIBLING DIFFERENCES IN YEARS OF EDUCATION BY COGNITIVE CLASS, 1994

Cognitive Class	n	Mean Difference in Years of Education
Very Bright siblings (90th + centile)	109	+ 1.9
Bright siblings (75th–89th)	266	+ 1.3
Normal reference group (25th–74th)	850	(Mean = 13.5 yrs., Std. dev. = 2.0)
Dull siblings (10th–24th)	326	− .8
Very Dull siblings (less than 10th)	149	− 1.6

SOURCE: NLSY.

with both biological parents at least through the younger sibling's seventh year.[7] These constraints produced a sample of 3,802 individuals who comprised 2,859 unique sibling pairs.

A variety of ways may be used to analyze the resulting sample. In this monograph, I use an expository method employing pairs in which one sibling had an IQ that fell in the normal range (embracing the 25th through the 74th centiles, or an IQ of approximately 90 through 109) and the other sibling fell in one of the other cognitive classes. A total of 1,074 sibling pairs met this requirement.

The Normals serve as the reference group. The analyses are based on paired comparisons in which the dependent variable is Y_c-Y_r, the difference between the value for the comparison sibling and the reference sibling in each pair.

This procedure left a sample of matched pairs with the characteristics shown in table 4–1.

As table 4–1 indicates, all four of the comparison groups have interpretable sample sizes, which will vary from analysis to analysis because of missing data for some of the variables in question. In all cases, computations of means and standard deviations for the reference group are limited to cases in which data are available for the comparison sibling.

I use this sample to examine how differences in IQ among siblings affect three variables that are directly related to earned income—educational attainment, occupation, and weeks worked—and then examine the relationship of IQ differences to earned income itself.

Educational Attainment. As of 1994, the mean years of education for a member of the Normal reference group was 13.5. Table 4–2 shows differences in mean years of education for the brighter and duller siblings.

Same household, same parents, different IQs—and markedly different educational careers. The typical Normal had 1.6 years more education than his Very Dull sibling and 1.9 years less education than his Very Bright sibling. These differences in mean years of education translate into wide differences in the probability of getting a college degree, as shown in table 4–3.

Among the Normals in the 1,009 sibling pairs with complete data on educational attainment, 811, or 80 percent, did not get a bachelor's degree. In the first pair of columns in the table, the Normals' percentage is therefore zero. Fifty-nine percent of the Very Bright siblings of those 811 Normals achieved what their less-bright sibling did not, as did almost 42 percent of the Brights. Meanwhile, only a handful of the Normals' less-bright siblings managed to get a B.A. when their Normal sibling had not.

Turning to the 198 Normals in the reference group who did obtain a bachelor's degree, 91 percent of their Very Bright siblings and 76 percent of their Bright siblings also completed college. The success rate for their Dull siblings was drastically lower (18 percent), while none of their Very Dull siblings completed college.

Altogether, among the 228 sibling pairs in which the reference and comparison sibling had different outcomes (one got a B.A. and the other did not), the B.A. went to the sibling with the higher IQ in 88 percent of the cases. Given the wage premium associated with college degrees, it should come as no surprise if we subsequently find that wages are also associated with sibling differences in IQ.

Occupational Attainment. At ages twenty-eight through thirty-six as of 1993, many of the NLSY subjects had not yet reached their mature career positions. Some who are now clerks will become managers; some who are now junior executives will become senior executives. Some will change careers altogether. Even at this point, however, the distinctions by cognitive class are substan-

TABLE 4–3
PERCENTAGE OF SIBLINGS IN EACH COGNITIVE CLASS ATTAINING THE BACHELOR'S DEGREE, 1994

Cognitive Class	For Reference Siblings without a B.A.		For Reference Siblings with a B.A.	
	n	Percentage of comparison siblings with a B.A.	n	Percentage of comparison siblings with a B.A.
Very Bright siblings (90th + centile)	75	58.7	46	91.3
Bright siblings (75th–89th)	220	41.8	78	75.6
Normal reference group (25th–74th)	811	(0)	198	(100)
Dull siblings (10th–24th)	339	1.2	55	18.2
Very Dull siblings (less than 10th)	177	0.6	19	0

SOURCE: NLSY.

tial. Table 4–4 shows differences in scores on the Duncan scale for measuring occupational prestige.

Score differences of these magnitudes translate into obvious differences in occupation. Of those who reported having an occupation in the 1994 interview, fewer than 1 percent of the Normals were in a profession (persons with advanced degrees who were lawyers, physicians, accountants, engineers, architects, scientists, and college professors in the arts and sciences), compared with 12 percent of their Very Bright siblings, 3 percent of the Brights, 0.3 percent of the Dulls, and none of the Very Dulls.

Education constrains occupational choices, so the overall occupational outcomes for the siblings are not surprising. It is predictable, for example, that Very Bright siblings are much more likely than Normals to be in managerial or professional positions, because most such jobs require at least a college degree, and the Bright and Very

TABLE 4–4

SIBLING DIFFERENCES IN SCORES FOR OCCUPATIONAL PRESTIGE BY COGNITIVE CLASS, 1993

Cognitive Class	n	Mean Difference Duncan Score Points
Very Bright siblings (90th + centile)	94	+ 10.9
Bright siblings (75th–89th)	234	+ 4.1
Normal reference group (25th–74th)	691	(Mean = 42.7, Std. dev. = 21.5)
Dull siblings (10th–24th)	261	− 10.4
Very Dull siblings (less than 10th)	102	− 18.0

SOURCE: NLSY.
NOTE: Sample is limited to those in which both siblings reported an occupation in 1994.

Bright siblings are much more likely to have obtained such a degree. Table 4–5 shows what happens when we limit the sample to sibling pairs who had attained the same general level of education.

The breakdown continues to show a role for IQ in determining occupational status even within groups of siblings that did and did not get B.A.s. The magnitude of the differences is reduced, however, remaining most conspicuous in the discrepancy between the Normals and their Very Dull siblings.

The reduction in the Duncan score differences among the upper three classes can be interpreted as meaning that most of the effect of IQ on occupational attainment is mediated by education. (In the case of sibling pairs that did not complete a B.A., the Bright siblings actually had a mean Duncan score 1.7 points lower than their Normal reference siblings.) The reduction could also reflect self-selection influences: a person with a Normal IQ who nonetheless completes a B.A., something only one out of five of his counterparts achieves, is probably exhibiting traits that are likely to affect occupational attainment positively. A person with a Very Bright IQ who nonetheless fails to complete a B.A., something that about three-quarters of his counterparts achieve, is probably exhibiting traits that are likely to work against high occupational attainment. In the absence of data for deciding between these alternative explanations, the safest assumption is that both factors are at work to unknown degrees.

Weeks Worked. Apart from occupation, how do the siblings compare in their success in getting and holding a job? Table 4–6 shows mean weeks of work in calendar year 1993.

When all the sibling pairs are examined (the first two columns of figures in table 4–6), the top two cognitive

TABLE 4–5
DIFFERENCES IN OCCUPATIONAL PRESTIGE AMONG THE COGNITIVE CLASSES, FOR SIBLING PAIRS WITH AND WITHOUT A COLLEGE DEGREE, 1993

Cognitive Class	n	Mean Difference in Duncan Score Points
For sibling pairs in which both had completed at least a B.A.:		
Very Bright siblings (90th + centile)	32	+ 7.6
Bright siblings (75th–89th)	46	+ 3.7
Normal reference group (25th–74th)	87	(Mean = 58.0, Std. dev. = 16.7)
Dull siblings (10th–24th)	9	− 12.3
Very Dull siblings (less than 10th)	0	—
For sibling pairs in which neither had completed a B.A.:		
Very Bright siblings (90 + centile)	21	+ 3.4
Bright siblings (75th–89th)	92	− 1.7
Normal reference group (25th–74th)	395	(Mean = 37.4, Std. dev. = 21.0)
Dull siblings (10th–24th)	198	− 7.6
Very Dull siblings (less than 10th)	84	− 16.0

SOURCE: NLSY.
NOTE: Sample is limited to those in which both siblings reported an occupation in 1994.

TABLE 4–6
SIBLING DIFFERENCES IN WEEKS WORKED BY COGNITIVE CLASS, 1993

Cognitive Class	All Sibling Pairs		Pairs in Which Both Siblings Were in the Labor Force All Year	
	n	Mean difference in no. of weeks worked	n	Mean difference in no. of weeks worked
Very Bright siblings (90th + centile)	106	+2.4	61	+.7
Bright siblings (75th–89th)	255	+2.2	129	–.3
Normal reference group (25th–74th)	815	(Mean = 42.5; Std. dev. = 17.3)	371	(Mean = 51.2; Std. dev. = 4.7)
Dull siblings (10th–24th)	313	–3.7	137	–1.9
Very Dull siblings (less than 10th)	141	–9.7	44	–.9

SOURCE: NLSY.

classes showed a moderate difference of more than two extra weeks worked compared with their Normal siblings. The large changes affected the Dulls and, especially, the Very Dulls, who worked almost ten weeks less than did their Normal siblings. As the last two columns of figures show, however, almost all of this discrepancy is explained by differences in availability for the labor force. When we limit the sibling pairs to those who reported that they were in the labor force throughout the year, the main finding is that almost everyone was employed almost all the time, no matter what his cognitive class. Perhaps this result reflects nothing more than a tendency for those who were unemployed to say instead that they were out of the labor force, but it could also point to an important leveling factor that cuts across IQ groups—that the attitudes and qualities other than IQ that lead one to remain in the labor force are associated with high employability.

Annual Earnings. The earnings data follow naturally. If brighter siblings get more education, have higher-level occupations, and are employed more of the time, they are going to make more money. They did, as shown in table 4–7.

In 1993, the median earnings for the Normals was $22,000. Their Very Bright siblings already earned a median of $11,500 more, while their Very Dull siblings earned $9,750 less. The Brights and Dulls each fell somewhere in between.

These are large differences. Think of them in terms of a family reunion in 1993, with one sibling belonging to each cognitive class, all sitting around the dinner table, all in their late twenties to mid-thirties, comparing their radically different courses in the world of work. Very few families have five siblings so arranged, of course, but the imaginative exercise serves to emphasize that we are not comparing apples and oranges here—not suburban white

TABLE 4–7
SIBLING DIFFERENCES IN EARNED INCOME BY COGNITIVE CLASS, 1993

Cognitive Class	n	Difference in Earnings, in 1993 Dollars	
		Mean	Median
Very Bright siblings (90th + centile)	99	+17,786	+11,500
Bright siblings (75th–89th)	257	+4,407	+4,000
Normal reference group (25th–74th)	779	(Mean = 23,703; Std. dev. = 18,606)	(Median = 22,000)
Dull siblings (10th–24th)	295	−5,792	−5,000
Very Dull siblings (less than 10th)	128	−9,462	−9,750

SOURCE: NLSY.

children with inner-city black children, not the sons of lawyers with the sons of ditchdiggers—but siblings, children of the same parents, who spent their childhoods under the same roof. They differed in their scores on a paper-and-pencil mental test.

5

How Much Difference Does It Make Whether the Analysis Controls for Parental SES or Compares Siblings?

ow much difference does it make whether one uses a sample of siblings, as in the results just presented, or uses a control for socioeconomic background, as in the results that opened the monograph?

In table 3–1, I presented the regression results from the full NLSY sample when *The Bell Curve's* parental SES index was entered along with IQ as an independent variable. That analysis indicated that an extra IQ point was associated with $462 of extra earned income, independent of parental SES. With the sibling analysis, how big is the effect? Table 5–1 gives an idea. For each sibling pair, a new variable was computed in which the income difference, $Income_C - Income_R$, was divided by the IQ difference, $IQ_C - IQ_R$. The resulting quotient represents the dollars associated with each IQ point of difference. The quotients reported in table 5–1, ranging from $420 to $892, surround the $462 figure obtained using the full NLSY sample and the parental SES index as the control for family background. We may produce a more direct

TABLE 5–1
THE DOLLAR VALUE OF AN EXTRA IQ POINT, BY COGNITIVE CLASS, 1993

Cognitive Class	n	Mean Dollars per IQ Point $\left(\dfrac{Income_C - Income_R}{IQ_C - IQ_R}\right)$
Very Bright siblings (90th+ centile)	99	892
Bright siblings (75th–89th)	257	420
Normal reference group (25th–74th)	779	(Mean = 23,703; Std. dev. = 18,606)
Dull siblings (10th–24th)	295	709
Very Dull siblings (less than 10th)	128	453

SOURCE: NLSY.

comparison by taking the entire sample of siblings (3,802 individuals, comprising 2,859 unique sibling pairs) and running two regression equations. In the first, the 3,802 individuals are treated as unrelated subjects, and the independent effect of IQ on earned income is computed after entering the parental SES index into the equation. In the second, the sample consists of the 2,859 sibling pairs, the dependent variable is the sibling difference in earned income, and the sole independent variable is the sibling difference in IQ. The former equation produces a coefficient for IQ of $446. The latter produces a coefficient for IQ of $453. *The Bell Curve*'s method of controlling for SES and the sibling method of controlling for everything in the family background yield interpretations of the independent role of IQ on income that are substantively indistinguishable.

This has been an expository presentation of data in

the sibling sample, not a technical one. Readers probably have many questions. For example, I have in effect presented the results for one column of a matrix, the one in which the Normals are the reference group. But one could also select all the Very Brights as a reference group and use their less bright siblings as the comparisons—and so on for each of the five cognitive classes. One might ask how parental SES differs for different combinations of pairs, or how regression to the mean might affect the analyses of sibling differences. This is not the place to explore these issues in detail, but in any case, Korenman and Winship, who conducted the sibling reanalysis of *The Bell Curve* mentioned earlier, already offer a more rigorous point of comparison.[8] They show the regression coefficient for IQ when the sibling sample is analyzed using *The Bell Curve*'s index of parental SES as a control variable, and again when the sibling sample is analyzed using each family as its own control.[9] The variables they used that correspond most closely to the ones used here were annual wages of year-round workers, years of schooling, attainment of a bachelors degree, being in a high-IQ occupation, males out of the labor force for more than one month, and males unemployed for more than one month. Table 5–2 presents the results of their analysis.

In the two sets of analyses, the coefficients for IQ were only fractionally different for any of these six outcome variables. In explaining economic success, the results using *The Bell Curve*'s SES index as a control for family background and a method using siblings—a much different method from the one I have presented—once again yielded substantively indistinguishable results.

At this juncture, it is well to emphasize that the sibling results do *not* demonstrate that socioeconomic status, or family background more generally, is unimportant in determining earned income. Whether one grows up in a rich family, whether two parents are in the house, whether one goes to church as a child, whether one's par-

TABLE 5–2
COMPARISON OF THE INDEPENDENT EFFECT OF IQ IN THE
SIBLING SAMPLE USING *THE BELL CURVE*'S CONTROL FOR
PARENTAL SES VERSUS A FIXED-EFFECT MODEL

Indicator	Bell Curve *Control for Parental SES*		Siblings Fixed-*Effects Model*	
	n	OLS or logit coefficient[a]	n	OLS or logit coefficient[a]
Annual earnings, year-round workers	1,579	5,548 (603)	1,579	5,317 (852)
Years of schooling	4,758	.59 (.02)	4,578	.45 (.02)
Attainment of BA	3,884	1.76 (.09)	309	1.87 (.23)
High-IQ occupation[b]	2,946	1.39 (.14)	94	1.72 (.43)
Out of labor force 1+ month[c]	1,096	−.34 (.10)	132	−.30 (.19)
Unemployed 1+ month[c]	720	−.52 (.14)	65	−.47 (.29)

a. Standard error in parentheses.
b. Includes accountants, architects, engineers, college teachers, mathematicians, natural and social scientists, physicians and dentists, and lawyers.
c. Men.
SOURCE: Adapted from S. Korenman and C. Winship, *A Reanalysis of* The Bell Curve: *Intelligence, Family Background, and Schooling,* Harvard University and National Bureau of Economic Research, revised August 1996, table 2.

ents are well-educated—the list could go on—might all have large effects on earnings as adults. The sibling analysis simply gives us a way of pushing these factors out of the picture and asking whether differences in IQ still make a difference among children from the same family. Obviously, they do.

6

The Utopian Sample

How much difference would it make if, magically, every child in the country could be given the same environmental advantages as the more fortunate of our children? This concluding chapter provides a way of thinking about the answer.

The Terms of Debate

The question of "how much difference it would make" is one of the most highly charged in the current policy debate, attracting impassioned editorials, television news features, and even a book by the nation's First Lady, all arguing that government interventions can dramatically improve a child's life chances. Some of the most virulent attacks on *The Bell Curve* were prompted by its cautions on this score.

Given the tendency for polarization, perhaps I should begin with common ground: no one doubts that, if all children had the advantages of the most fortunate, some narrowing of inequalities would occur. The environment in which a child is raised does make a difference. The question is not *whether* but *how much*.

In academia, the controversy over what "some narrowing" means, and the controversy over *The Bell Curve* itself, is being played out via two very different traditions. The first is the sociological tradition. The Korenman and Winship paper is an example. After the sibling analysis, which yields results very similar to those presented in *The Bell Curve,* the authors embark on analyses that add many more independent variables to the regression equations, put the data through transformations that the authors consider appropriate, and conclude that family background variables, interpreted as environmentally manipulable variables, are much more important than Herrnstein and I thought.[10] The happy implication of such analyses is that the right social policies can drastically narrow the variation in social and economic success.

The other tradition is identified with psychometrics and genetics. It assumes that the child's development is a combination of environmental and genetically transmitted characteristics. Thus, for example, it sees high parental income not simply as a socioeconomic characteristic, but also as an expression of parental traits (including IQ) that are part of the child's genetic heritage. Illegitimacy is a less obvious case in point. Illegitimacy helps explain life outcomes independently of the child's IQ. But women who have babies out of wedlock also have IQs that average 15 points lower than those of women who do not. The effects that sociologists tend to attribute to "being born to an unmarried mother" are in part attributable to genetically transmitted characteristics that are not susceptible to manipulation. From this perspective, *The Bell Curve*'s SES index (or any such index) may be criticized for overestimating the importance of environmental factors.[11] To add still more confounded "environmental" variables to the list of independent variables only compounds the error.

This tradition is represented by a large literature on adoption that includes, but extends far beyond, the famous studies of identical twins raised apart, and by a rapidly growing literature on siblings and half siblings. An analysis bearing directly on *The Bell Curve* has been conducted by David C. Rowe and his colleagues at the University of Arizona.[12] It concludes that the greater part of inequality in education and income in the NLSY sibling sample was attributable to genes, with the shared environment playing a subordinate role.

The qualification in that sentence, the *shared* environment, points to a recent line of inquiry based on the concept of *non*shared environment. Rowe and Robert Plomin have been leading figures in this growing literature.[13] Children growing up in the same household only partially share the same environment. The sources of difference include some of the obvious possibilities—the different ways parents treat their children, or differences in their educational experience even though they attend the same schools. Other sources of nonshared environment might be events in utero, accidents that occur to one child but not to another, or differences in friends. Many of the sources of nonshared environment are still mysterious. But although much remains to be learned, it seems increasingly clear that even when environmental factors are at issue, the role of nonshared environment dominates that of shared environment in explaining behavioral development. Or to put it in policy terms: whatever role the environment plays, only a relatively small part of that role lends itself to targeted manipulation through social interventions, and this realization must moderate expectations about the plausible range of effects that we might obtain by social interventions intended to affect that amorphous thing called the "environment."

I applaud efforts on all sides to achieve greater precision in calibrating the narrowing in outcomes that might theoretically be achieved. Let me suggest, however, that the sibling data already give us ample reason to conclude that no matter how successful the attempts to improve the lot of the less advantaged might be, American society is going to be left with extremely large inequalities. Let me illustrate this by creating what I will call the *utopian sample.*

The NLSY's Fortunate Children

I presented the data from the sibling sample as if it simply provided a cleaner way of controlling for family background. In reality, it did much more. To ensure that both children had at least the same shared family environment, it was appropriate that I limit the pairs to full biological siblings who lived in the same household for at least the first seven years of the younger sibling's life. But in applying that condition, the sample selection procedure had the effect of disqualifying all children who were born to single mothers or whose parents divorced early. In other words, the sibling sample represented a population in which all parents were wed before the child was born and all young children were brought up by both parents during their most formative years.

Such a population is one that has already achieved much of what we ideally want to achieve through social policy. If I had begun this monograph by saying I was going to compare earned income among people who had grown up in intact families versus the population at large, most readers would have taken for granted that the youths from the intact families would do better, regardless of IQ.

The obvious next question is, What would America look like if all children grew up in intact families? Instead of concentrating on differences between siblings, as in the analyses just presented, why not go back to the entire NLSY sample and select that subset of subjects who meet the same condition—growing up with both biological parents from birth through age seven—that we imposed on the sibling sample? And why not carry the process a step further? Having already created a sample without illegitimacy and early divorce, let us slay the greatest of all the social policy *bêtes noires,* poverty. To achieve that, I lop off all subjects whose parents were anywhere in the bottom 25 percent of the income distribution as of 1978–1979. This produces a sample of 3,908 NLSY youths who grew up in households which, by 1978–1979, had a median parental income of $50,000 and a minimum income of $25,800 (1993 dollars).[14]

The sample is utopian not just because it has virtually no illegitimacy, divorce, or poverty. The way in which it has been selected has also necessarily effected drastic improvements in the educational system in which the youths grew up (the utopian sample is highly selected for parents living in neighborhoods with good schools). The utopian sample youths had a big edge in their potential access to college, both economically and because the sample is highly selected for the kind of parents who actively encourage their children to continue their educations. The same selection factors mean that we have created a population in which the incidence of good health care, childhood nutrition, and nurturing home environments are all extremely high as compared with the population at large.

Surely it goes without saying that this subsample will show narrowing of social and economic outcomes in comparison with the population at large. The first-order correlations between income and such outcomes are too large to expect anything else. But before looking at the following data, perhaps it would be useful for readers to ask themselves how large they expect the effects to be. No poverty, no illegitimacy, no early family breakup: how much difference do you expect it to make in the next generation?

First-Generation Outcomes in the Utopian Sample

Education is a good place to start. If we can keep families together and put everyone above the poverty line, will we demonstrate how arbitrarily college educations have been distributed in the United States? Table 6–1 shows the success of the members of the utopian sample in educational attainment. The results are shown alongside the comparable figures for the entire NLSY sample, using

TABLE 6-1
EDUCATIONAL ATTAINMENT IN THE UTOPIAN SAMPLE, BY COGNITIVE CLASS, 1994

Cognitive Class	Mean Years of Education		Percentage Obtaining a B.A.	
	Utopian sample	Full NLSY sample	Utopian sample	Full NLSY sample
Very Bright (90th + centile)	16.5	16.5	80	77
Bright (75th–89th)	15.2	15.0	57	50
Normal (25th–74th)	13.4	13.2	19	16
Dull (10th–24th)	12.3	11.9	4	3
Very Dull (less than 10th)	11.4	10.9	1	1

SOURCE: NLSY.

TABLE 6–2
WEEKS WORKED IN THE UTOPIAN SAMPLE,
BY COGNITIVE CLASS, 1993

	Mean Weeks Worked	
	---	---
Cognitive Class	Utopian sample	Full NLSY sample
Very Bright (90th + centile)	45.6	45.4
Bright (75th–89th)	45.1	45.2
Normal (25th–74th)	43.0	41.8
Dull (10th–24th)	39.0	36.5
Very Dull (less than 10th)	35.8	30.7

SOURCE: NLSY.

sample weights to compute results that are representative of the national population ages twenty-eight through thirty-six. In this and the following tables, sample sizes for all the cognitive classes are in the hundreds or larger.

The differences between the utopian sample and the national population are startlingly small. The youths in the utopian sample came from families that were overwhelmingly likely to support college enthusiastically and have the financial wherewithal to help. But the odds that someone in the Normal group would get a B.A. rose only from about 16 to 19 percent. The "big" effect in table 6–1 is that the odds that a Bright subject would get a B.A. rose from 50 percent all the way to 57 percent. Being from the utopian sample made virtually no difference in the college prospects of Dull or Very Dull youths. It did help them stay in school an extra half year or so, on the average; that's all.

The story for weeks worked in 1993 is shown in table 6–2. Coming from an intact family in the upper 75 per-

TABLE 6–3
EARNED INCOME FOR THE UTOPIAN SAMPLE,
BY COGNITIVE CLASS, 1993

| | Median Earned Income (dollars) | |
| | | |
Cognitive Class	Utopian sample	Full NLSY sample
Very Bright		
(90th + centile)	38,000	36,000
Bright (75th—89th)	27,000	27,000
Normal (25th–74th)	23,000	21,000
Dull (10th–24th)	16,000	13,000
Very Dull		
(less than 10th)	11,000	7,500

SOURCE: NLSY.

cent of the income distribution had the effect of modestly increasing the weeks worked by the Dull and the Very Dull, by 2.5 weeks and 5.1 weeks respectively, but it left them well behind the weeks worked by their brighter counterparts. The effects of being in the utopian sample on the Brights and Very Brights was effectively nil.

The income results for the utopian sample are shown in table 6–3. If there is one indicator on which the children of the utopian sample might be expected to show consistent and substantial advantage over the children in the general population, it is in earned income. This should hold true whether one is reasoning from the right (children who grow up in intact families will have a major advantage in their socialization to the workplace and in their habits of responsibility and industry) or from the left (children who grow up in families with money do better than children who grow up poor). And yet the median earnings of the Very Bright subjects from the utopian sample were only 6 percent higher than for the full NLSY sample. For the Brights, median earnings were identical in the utopian and full samples. The Normals in the utopian sample averaged 10 percent higher than those in the full sample. The utopian Dulls' advantage was 23 percent. The big difference is in the median earned income of the Very Dulls in the utopian sample, $11,000—47 percent higher than the $7,500 for the full NLSY sample.

Family Formation, Fertility, and Intergenerational Forces for Dispersion

The first-generation results from the utopian sample lead to an obvious question: if the below-average-IQ offspring of intact, nonpoor families fall so far short of their parents' economic success, what happens in the second generation? Return to the one success story involving median earnings for the Very Dulls. Despite making 47 percent more than the Very Dulls in the population at large, fully 27 percent of the utopian Very Dulls were below the poverty line even after adding in welfare income and spousal income. Eleven percent of the utopian Dulls were below the poverty line. If we observe poverty go from zero in the parents' generation to 11 and 27 percent poverty in the below-average-IQ children's generation, the implication is that within two or three generations the income dispersion—the level of inequality—will be back where it started.

One might reach this conclusion simply by extrapolating from the income dispersion observed in the first generation after the utopian condition. We can do better than that, however, by examining collateral indicators.

Marriage and Divorce. In the top three cognitive classes, similar proportions (76–79 percent) of those in the utopian sample had gotten married, whether Normal, Bright, or Very Bright. But only 70 percent of the Dulls and 69 percent of the Very Dulls had married. A parallel story applies to divorce. The divorce ratio in the first five years of marriage ranged from 34 to 39 percent for the top three cognitive classes. It was 47 percent for the Dulls and 49 percent for the Very Dulls.[15]

Add to this the phenomenon known as "assortative mating"—likes marry likes. High-IQ people tend to marry each other, and so do low-IQ people. As a result, the spouses of the smart who work make more than the spouses of the not-smart. For example, the spouses of the Very Dulls who worked had a median earned income of $15,500, while the spouses of the Very Brights who worked had a median earned income of $30,500.

Combine these mutually reinforcing patterns, and they make a big difference in the expected family earned income by cognitive class, as shown in table 6-4.

The gap in earned income reported in table 6–4 widens substantially because of the different marriage patterns among siblings in different cognitive classes. Notice also that using family earned income as the measure further diminishes the advantage shown by the children with average and below average IQs in the utopian sample. The advantage of the utopian Normals shrinks to 2 percent over the Normals in the population at large; the advantage of the utopian Dulls shrinks to 7 percent. The advantage of the utopian Very Dulls remains large, but is reduced to 42 percent.[16]

Illegitimacy. To the degree that family formation makes a difference independent of IQ and one is trying to predict the further dispersion of outcomes in successive generations, it is relevant to ask about the family circumstances into which the next generation will be born. I have already noted that marriage declined and divorce increased for the least intelligent of the siblings in the utopian sample. Combined with childbearing behavior, these produced major differences in the percentages of children born out of wedlock to the members of the utopian sample, as shown in table 6–5.

TABLE 6-4
AUGMENTING INCOME THROUGH A SPOUSE'S EARNINGS IN THE UTOPIAN SAMPLE, BY COGNITIVE CLASS, 1993

Cognitive Class	Percentage with a Spouse Who Has Earned Income		Median Earned Family Income	
	Utopian sample	Full NLSY sample	Utopian sample	Full NLSY sample
Very Bright (90th + centile)	58	58	53,700	53,000
Bright (75th–89th)	61	59	47,200	45,000
Normal (25th–74th)	53	54	37,750	37,000
Dull (10th–24th)	38	39	25,000	23,400
Very Dull (less than 10th)	30	27	17,000	12,000

SOURCE: NLSY.

TABLE 6–5
ILLEGITIMACY AMONG WOMEN IN THE UTOPIAN SAMPLE,
BY COGNITIVE CLASS, 1994

	Children Born out of Wedlock (percent)	
Cognitive Class	Utopian sample	Full NLSY sample
Very Bright (90th+ centile)	3	5
Bright (75th–89th)	6	6
Normal (25th–74th)	14	14
Dull (10th–24th)	33	32
Very Dull (less than 10th)	49	50

SOURCE: NLSY.

In the utopian sample, effectively all of the parental generation had been married. In the next generation, almost half of the children of the Very Dull and a third of the children of the Dull—figures within a few percentage points of those in the full NLSY sample—are being born to unmarried women, compared with 3 percent of the children of the Very Bright and 6 percent of the children of the Bright. This is another force working toward dispersion of outcomes in the subsequent generation.

Demography. The variance of outcomes in the next generation is also going to be affected by the comparative numbers of children who will be brought up in families of the various cognitive classes. Table 6–6 reports the situation as of 1994.

Demographers will find it gloomily interesting that the average age at which the utopian Very Dull women give birth was 4.6 years younger than for the Very Bright ones, and the number of children born to Very Dull

TABLE 6–6
CHILDBEARING CHARACTERISTICS OF WOMEN IN THE UTOPIAN
SAMPLE, BY COGNITIVE CLASS, 1994

Cognitive Class	Fertility to Date		Mother's Mean Age at Birth	
	Utopian sample	Full NLSY sample	Utopian sample	Full NLSY sample
Very Bright (90th + centile)	1.0	1.0	29.0	28.5
Bright (75th–89th)	1.3	1.4	27.4	27.1
Normal (25th–74th)	1.4	1.6	26.0	25.2
Dull (10th–24th)	1.7	1.9	24.5	23.7
Very Dull (less than 10th)	2.1	2.3	24.4	22.8

SOURCE: NLSY.

women averaged a full child more than for the Very
Brights.[17] The combination of total number of children
and the ages at which they are born determines the ex-
tent of what is known as "differential fertility." The advantaged youths represented in the utopian sample are
giving birth to a cohort that is going to be drawn much
more heavily from the lower end of the cognitive distribution than from the high end. This not only points to a
situation in which inequality in the utopian sample re-
verts to the levels in the population at large; it opens the
possibility of a future in which IQ's role will tend to produce larger inequalities than we now observe. A detailed
discussion of how differential fertility is playing out on
the national scene is given in *The Bell Curve,* chapter 15.

The Thin Edge of the Wedge. Returning to the current
generation, one final point needs emphasis. Great as the

income inequalities in the utopian sample are, they are not nearly as great as they are going to be in another ten or fifteen years. The income trajectory for low-skill occupations peaks early, while the income trajectory for professionals and senior managers peaks late. The differences in earned income as of 1993, when the NLSY subjects were aged twenty-eight through thirty-six, will get much larger. The incomes of the most successful in business and the professions may be expected to increase for another two decades. The incomes of those in low-skill jobs cannot continue to decline indefinitely, but neither is there any reason to think that they will increase substantially. Look once again at table 6–3, showing current inequality in income even within the utopian sample, do some mental estimates of where those differences are likely to be in twenty years, and then ponder how those sustained differences in income will translate into inequality in net worth.

A Common Policy Challenge

Taking everything together, the prospect conveyed by the utopian sample is for very large differences in both income and social behavior, intertwined with systematically different distributions of intelligence at the various income levels—all of which amounts to the kind of cognitive stratification that *The Bell Curve* described. And these are levels of inequality produced by the offspring of a population more advantaged in jobs, income, and marital stability than even the most starry-eyed social reformer can hope to achieve.

These results are what we obtain after simulating utterly unreachable success. In the real world, experience gives no confidence (putting it charitably) that activist social policy can even reduce the number of children growing up in poverty, illegitimacy, and divorce, let alone end such problems. On the contrary, experience reveals that these problems have remained static or gotten worse in the eras of the most active attempts to reduce them. Experience gives no confidence that social services can counteract the effects of a bad family environment. On the contrary, recent research is filled with studies showing how intractable these environments seem to be. Less charitably, some observers, of whom I am one, think a case can be made that activist social policy exacerbates the problems it seeks to ameliorate. But it is not necessary to hold that view to join in this minimalist conclusion: no realistic assessment of our empirical experience in using social interventions to reduce social problems can yield grounds for concluding that our repertoire of social interventions, augmented with greater funding and energy, may be expected to narrow the national income inequality statistics. Nor does one see on the horizon any breakthroughs in the science of engineering human behavior that are likely to change the situation.

People of different political viewpoints may legitimately respond to such data with policy prescriptions that are in polar opposition. In many ways, the left has the easier task. These data are tailor-made for the conclusion that a Rawlsian redistributive state is the only answer. If we do not yet know how to solve social problems by manipulating behavior, we can nonetheless eliminate poverty by giving poor people enough money to lift everyone out of poverty. But if the left is to adopt this solution, it must reconcile its position with what is happening to economic growth and to unemployment in the European societies that have pursued income redistribution most vigorously.

For its part, the right must state forthrightly why it thinks that a free society that tolerates large differences in outcomes is preferable to an authoritarian society that reduces them. This requires a thoughtful inquiry into the relationship between inequality and the "happiness of the people," to use Madison's phrase, that few on the contemporary right have yet undertaken.

In the meantime, it seems fair to conclude from

these data that, though the answers may be different for those of competing political persuasions, the challenge is common to all. For many years now, too many scholars on left and right alike have pretended they live in a Lake Wobegon world where everyone can be above average. It is time for policy analysts to stop avoiding the reality of human inequality, a reality that neither equalization of opportunity nor a freer market will circumvent.

Notes

1. R. J. Herrnstein and C. Murray, *The Bell Curve: Intelligence and Class Structure in American Life* (New York: The Free Press, 1994).

2. The cutoff points for the top and bottom classes in *The Bell Curve* were set at the 5th and 95th centiles. In the sibling analyses that follow in this monograph, using the 5th and 95th centiles produces small and unstable sample sizes; hence the expansion of the top and bottom classes to include the top and bottom deciles of the population. In this monograph as in *The Bell Curve,* the middle of the five classes is deliberately set to include half the population, reflecting our contention that the most important relationships between IQ and economic and social phenomena occur at the tails of the distribution. This is not intended to reflect a specific hypothesis of nonlinearity, but to focus attention on the large differences that characterize groups at the tails of the distribution.

3. The NLSY systematically oversampled blacks, Hispanics, and low-income whites. It also provides sample weights so that analyses can produce nationally representative estimates. It is a matter of technical debate whether these weights should be used in computing correlations or regression coefficients. The policy throughout this monograph is to use sampling weights when presenting medians or means for the full NLSY sample, so as to provide the best estimate of the nationally representative figure, but not to use sampling weights when calculating correlations or regressions. Sampling weights are not applied in any of the sibling analyses.

4. For a description of the index and its construction, see *The Bell Curve,* appendix 2.

5. A. J. Reiss, O. D. Duncan, P. K. Hatt, and C. C. North, *Occupations and Social Status* (Glencoe, Illinois: The Free Press, 1961).

6. Herrnstein and I did not try to adjudicate this issue in *The Bell Curve,* but we generally agreed with those who see measures of parental SES as being confounded with parental IQ. We assumed that our estimates of the independent effect

of IQ were conservative. See *The Bell Curve*, pp. 123–24 and 286–87.

7. More precisely, they believed themselves to be the children of the same biological parents. The NLSY coding distinguishes between sibling and step sibling or adoptive sibling. As an additional screen, I prepared profiles for each subject based on the question that asks whether the subject was living with his or her parents at various ages, requiring that both members of a sibling pair reported living with their parents at birth and that the older sibling had consistently reported living with both parents in all the years up to and including the birth year of the younger sibling. I used the same profiles of answers to determine whether both siblings had lived together through at least age seven of the younger sibling.

8. S. Korenman and C. Winship, "A Reanalysis of *The Bell Curve:* Intelligence, Family Background, and Schooling," Harvard University and National Bureau of Economic Research (rev. Aug. 1996).

9. "In the case of continuous outcomes (dependent variables), fixed-effect analysis amounts to entering a dummy variable for each family of origin. For dichotomous (binary) outcomes, we estimate fixed-effect logit models for the oldest pair of siblings from each baseline household." Korenman and Winship, "A Reanalysis," p. 9.

10. Another example is C. S. Fischer, M. Hout, M. S. Jankowski, S. R. Lucas, A. Swidler, and K. Voss, *Inequality by Design: Cracking the Bell Curve Myth* (Princeton, New Jersey: Princeton University Press, 1996).

11. See, for example, R. Plomin and C. S. Bergman, "The Nature of Nurture: Genetic Influence on 'Environmental' Measures," *Behavioral and Brain Sciences* 14 (1991): 373–427; and David C. Rowe, *The Limits of Family Influence: Genes, Experience, and Behavior* (New York: Guilford Press, 1994).

12. D. C. Rowe, W. J. Vesterdal, and J. L. Rodgers, "Herrnstein's Syllogism: Common Genetic and Shared Environmental Influences on IQ, Education, and Income," University of Arizona (1997).

13. In addition to the Plomin and Rowe books, see, for example, J. L. Rodgers and D. C. Rowe, "Does Contiguity Breed Similarity? A Within-Family Analysis of Nonshared Sources of IQ Differences between Siblings," *Developmental Psychology* 21 (1985): 743–46; L. H. Cyphers, D. W. Fulker, et al., "Cognitive Abilities in the Early School Years: No Effects of Shared Environment between Parents and Offspring," *Intelligence* 13 (1989): 369–86; and D. A. Grayson, "Twins Reared Together: Minimizing Shared Environmental Effects," *Behavior Genetics* 19 (1989): 593–608.

14. The NLSY does not provide parental incomes prior to 1978, but omitting the bottom 25 percent of the income distribution at a time when the percentage of persons under the poverty line (for persons in their thirties through early fifties) was only about 8 percent means that the proportion of parents who met my income criterion in the late 1970s but were in poverty during the siblings' upbringing is likely to be very small. Exactly how small cannot be determined with the data at hand.

15. For the full NLSY sample, the divorce rate rises curvilinearly from the Very Brights (32 percent) down through the Very Dulls (53 percent).

16. What happens if we use total family income from all sources? I have not focused on this in the text, because the topic is the independent effect of IQ, and "all sources" include both trust funds and welfare, neither of which is attributable to the ability of the recipient of the income. But are such payments (more often welfare than trust funds) enough to shrink income inequality? They have a substantial effect for the Very Dulls, raising the median family income for the entire NLSY population from $12,000 (earned income only) to $19,098 (total family income). They have less effect on the utopian sample, achieving an increase of the median from $18,000 to $23,180. These data do, however, reinforce the point made in the conclusion of the monograph: if one seeks to achieve income equality, then direct income redistribution, without trying to change the behavior of the poor, is the obvious choice.

17. This gap could close somewhat as the NLSY women complete their childbearing years, since high-IQ woman tend to have children later, but examination of births among the older NLSY women (who were as old as thirty-seven in 1994) suggests that the amount of closure will be very small.

About the Author

CHARLES MURRAY is the Bradley Fellow at the American Enterprise Institute. His books include *Losing Ground: American Social Policy 1950–1980, In Pursuit: Of Happiness and Good Government, What It Means to Be a Libertarian: A Personal Interpretation,* and, with the late Richard J. Herrnstein, *The Bell Curve: Intelligence and Class Structure in American Life.*

AEI STUDIES ON UNDERSTANDING ECONOMIC INEQUALITY
Marvin H. Kosters, series editor

ATTITUDES TOWARD ECONOMIC INEQUALITY
Everett Carll Ladd and Karlyn H. Bowman

COMPARING POVERTY: THE UNITED STATES AND OTHER
INDUSTRIAL NATIONS
McKinley L. Blackburn

THE DISTRIBUTION OF WEALTH: INCREASING INEQUALITY?
John C. Weicher

EARNINGS INEQUALITY: THE INFLUENCE OF CHANGING
OPPORTUNITIES AND CHOICES
Robert H. Haveman

INCOME INEQUALITY AND IQ
Charles Murray

INCOME MOBILITY AND THE MIDDLE CLASS
*Richard V. Burkhauser, Amy D. Crews,
Mary C. Daly, and Stephen P. Jenkins*

INCOME REDISTRIBUTION AND THE REALIGNMENT
OF AMERICAN POLITICS
*Nolan M. McCarty, Keith T. Poole,
and Howard Rosenthal*

RELATIVE WAGE TRENDS, WOMEN'S WORK,
AND FAMILY INCOME
Chinhui Juhn

THE THIRD INDUSTRIAL REVOLUTION: TECHNOLOGY,
PRODUCTIVITY, AND INCOME INEQUALITY
Jeremy Greenwood

WAGE INEQUALITY: INTERNATIONAL COMPARISONS
OF ITS SOURCES
Francine D. Blau and Lawrence M. Kahn